AT THE FRONTIER

At The Frontier

JULIAN ENNIS

HARRY CHAMBERS/PETERLOO POETS

First published in 1982
by Harry Chambers/Peterloo Poets
Treovis Farm Cottage, Upton Cross, Liskeard, Cornwall PL14 5BQ

ISBN 0 905291 42 5

Printed in Great Britain by
Latimer Trend & Company Ltd, Plymouth

ACKNOWLEDGEMENTS

Of the poems in this book which were not in *Cold Storage*, most have already appeared in the following periodicals:—*Anglo-Welsh Review, Ariel, Bananas, The Cornish Review, Country Life, Forum, London Welshman, The Month, Phoenix, Poetry Review, Outposts, Umbrella.*

Cover illustration: grateful acknowledgement is made to The Tate Gallery, London and to the Paul Nash Trust for permission to use "Pillar & Moon" by Paul Nash.

Harry Chambers/Peterloo Poets receives financial assistance from The Arts Council of Great Britain.

Contents

At The Frontier

Ahead, further than seeing, is martyred ground
Left to old growths, sacked walls,
The litter of relics.
You can hear only the murmuring
Of forsaken fields and shrines,
Feel only that you are being watched from tall towers,
And will retreat.

But you are still safe, here in your base camp.
And there is work to do before you start
The defiant journey home:
Descriptions to be made for posterity,
Signals sent to those who are imagining,
Rubbish to be burnt, the site swept and garnished,
Last indulgences.

And you can take comfort that, at whatever cost,
You did come, and made your mark.
You have, also, a clearer notion of what the place is like,
A picture in your mind.
And you know that someone is there,
Waiting beyond the lie of the land,
In the buttressed mystery,
And will not let you pass
Except you surrender, following his directions.

Either this or endless stalemate,
War for ever with one who will always lure you back;
And who, after all—there has been some evidence,
And much propaganda,
And you have often wondered—
May, the heroic years forgotten,
Next time, if you will advance,
Grasp your hand
And, with wine for your return,
Laughing the grim frontier away,
Astonish you with welcome.

Retirement Resort

Here they have come to their vision's ending,
Survivors from the hinterland,
Returned to water,
Their children haunting
An incredible future.

Here, in corralled bungalows,
Warding off the siren and the silence
Familiar as gulls,
They keep the vigil of windows,
Devise new rituals.

Here holiday-makers plunder
Their sacred pools, trespass on their sand,
Taunt them with time,
And, leaving them to winter,
Romance home.

Here, observing protocol, they parade
Downhill past the grim shrines
Lining the way
Towards the small, polite esplanade
And the great, barbaric sea.

Gates

If we turn left at the gates
We can take the by-pass smooth as cream
To the shoreline of our fancy,
Play on the forbidden fruit-machines,
Pose with donkeys,
Hitch our folk-wagons to the pier,
Gawk at mermaids in the sideshow tanks,
Or just beachcomb among the rocks
And listen to the roaring.

If we turn right at the gates
We can take the back street rough as coke
To the church where we should be,
Parade around the praying knights,
Offer up our small donations
To the restoration fund, smell the dust,
Commune with the painted angels,
Or just stroll among the saints
And listen to the silence.

So we prefer to remain here
Lying on the neat lines of grass
And watch the wall we do not dare go over.
Here, like birds, we find enough worms
To make any gate welcome.
For we seek the quiet life,
Content to listen to whatever sound
Is made by something somehow
Between the silence and the roaring.

Oxford Street, Winter

Snappily striding, cutting short capers,
Thousands of girly-longlegs pass below the eye-line,
Trimming time and the pavements away,
Weaving in to occupy the century.

But where do they go to in this winter-time?
To market for beauty preparations, sir;
To bed-squatter rooms, sir; to awkward parents;
To seek new possessions, sit at old desks;
To meet each other at the next station,
Out from home, far from the level crossing,
Every shopping day to the Christmas that always comes.
Only the colours matter, the speed and beat,
Truth and life along the swinging-skirted way.
Everywhere young, they fight with their faces to the show.

And so squares like me, Soho and Golden,
Bless them—often unawares—and are glad
When they visit us in the folded, sidestreet wings,
Spread their lunches over their gleaming knees,
And wait, silent with us in an old romance,
Lovers all, these mothers soon of men.

Wall Paintings

abandoned German gun-emplacements, the Calais coast

Over there, behind the clouds and the gulls,
The bluebird-singing cliffs waited, and then
All the stubborn, thatched mystery the men
Who lurked painting here tried to solve with shells:
Adlestrop and its birds in the dark north
Mocking with the waves and the pebble-dash.
So, between the thuds, challenged by whitewash,
They muralled days of victory and wrath,
Memorising a new Lascaux, until,
As the dawn chorused over Gloucestershire,
Abandoning their jokes on hopeless walls,
They fled, leaving in the defeat and dirt
Their caves to us who now come to the swill
Of rats and the darkness and the foul air
To shine our tourist torches on their art.

Prelude in the Pyrenees

High and cold in the mountains, I sat down
To hear the thunder bashing their white slopes
And watch the world spinning round with the clouds,
And an avalanche of sheep bleating back
To safety, taking the right direction,
The unseen shepherd shouting strange commands.
'Mère! Mère!', their bells clanging the alarm.

That morning I had finished my slow march
Through the vineyards lined up on parade,
And said goodbye to the black madonnas
Cuddling loaves in the mangers of their arms.
France was behind me, and all its sacraments.

And as I sat near heaven I remembered
The flocks in Lourdes and how the priests, with strange
Commands, pointed in the right direction.
I saw again the holidaying eyes
Bright with souvenirs, and I heard
'Ave, Maria!' clanging into space
From the rosaries of wobbling candles,
While all around me spun prayer-wheels of hope.

And I saw again—as I shall always
See—the one young woman who looked at me
Death's daggers, as though the fault were mine.
She had come to a grotto to live,
And I had tried to pray the miracle
Might happen there and then before my eyes,
And handed in a candle—so many francs—
To burn for her, and filled my flask with pure
Water to drink her on her feet.

By now, I supposed, she was dead. The sheep
Lived on, though: still they fell and flung their din
At the flashing, roaring summits. I stood
And cheered them on their way, and raised my cup
To drink his health, the unseen shepherd who,
With strange commands, had called them from the storm.

Pentecost

Voyaging back home from worship that day,
Taking for granted my sabbath county
That sped between the fire and the water,
Freed by the wind, a fair of bursting fields
With all its trees blossom-thick for passion,
I came, possessed of holy bread and wine,
To the memorial which told the place
Where death stood holding out his patient arms.
So, not failing, I passed the time of year
And promised never to forget, then strode
Into my valley risen from winter,
Swift and warm with swallows gleaming like saints.
And at sunset I led the earth in prayer,
And sang triumphant vespers with the owls.

A Drowned Village

Below this gleam, between these mounds, there once,
The oldest people say, lived a village,
Which, for some sin, was cursed and drowned to death.
What the sin had been the local fables—
The gossip, the scandal,—differed about.
The district archivist—the stirrer-up
Of discontent, enemy of progress—
Sighing (being short of breath) and shaking
His head (a nervous, family complaint),
Believed it was a refusal to hate
The beauty of the soil and the buildings,
To march with the times and accept the facts.
Others more spiritually minded—
The lunatic fringe, all of them on drugs—
Thought it was a stubborn faith in the wrong god,
And the new god, in his anger, had called
The river to its ancient vocation,
The parish pump sunk by the Water Board.
Perhaps the false deity was Bacchus,
And modern soldiers had gone to war,
Invaded the place and watered it down.
Perhaps he was Pan, and the same soldiers
Had judged it best the folk should play it cool.
Whatever the truth, the dwellers had paid
A high price for their secret wickedness.
The houses and the dancers, the postman,
The farm-workers, the schoolchildren, the church,
The store, the pub, the vicarage, had gone,
Without trace, flooded out of sight.
And it was a good thing too; for a town
Somewhere aloof thirsted with big new throats.

So, standing here, I think of a village
Which, after such time, had running water
And joined the main stream. Who is milking now
In the leaking shippons? Do the bats float
In the belfry, and are there poor cats
Hallowing the adage? And what wild weeds
Sit swaying and guzzling in the saloon?
Is there the churching of mermaids? What form
Of prayer is used for those in such peril?
What new monster waits to be a legend?

And I watch the long light of silence creep
Across the lake, unshaken by the wind;
And then, a stranger, I turn away,
Recalling the future. And as I trudge
Past the old men's beards hanging up to dry,
Through the wood where, in the early evening,
The roosters come to haunt another world,
Suddenly, beyond the wavelets, I hear
A distant hammering, as though someone
Were making a new faith, meaning to move
To a new home on earth. And I wish him luck,
And all that is his for life, two by two.

Abbey

They came first, in silent April,
To be apart with souls,
Returning, after sad centuries,
To new walls.
Nothing bombarded their village stillness;
Salvation seemed for ever.
Time would not yet raid their shy doors,
Scatter them to lost graves,
And bring the rich, swaggering lords.
The farm was still to be, and the vigil of ruins.

But long before the first saints, there were prayers.
And so now, while the world beyond,
Giant against giant,
Bangs again at their retreat,
Splashes the sky and pelts barns and towers,
No further off than a boy might sling stones,
The next sister, alone in the obstinate chapel,
Kneels on guard.

Missionaries

The earliest owners, our long shadows,
Left them alone to seed, saw their day-bloom,
Dreamt at night what quaint acts they danced,
And knew their songs and stories.

But then missionaries arrived, preaching cultivation,
Advising special earth for new breeds;
So they vied with strangers for trophies,
Button-holed them, feathered caps with them,
Cut them down to size, decorating rooms,
Paraphrased legends, wrote handbooks,
Organised societies, quoted Latin names,
Bequeathing us a clean, paved place.

Yet still wild images sprouted between the slabs.
Some loss was restless among the trim plants;
And our pink fingers itched to pluck out the plastic gnomes
And unweed our wonder.

And now we wait, straining to see odd shapes returning
And hear the garden sing and tell again.

Cosmonaut

At first I took it for a speck of dirt
Caught everywhere in the draught,
And I watched idly its jaunty flight,
And considered its lack of aim,
Its unwantedness, how it was left
To no devices, such freedom.

But then I saw that it lived and meant
All the skimming there and back
Across the blue window. Each movement
Of its wild legs, the fall and rise,
Was a huge heaving, a strain to take
A grip on things, make sense of so much space.

I marvelled at this urge through air,
The seeming sureness, the pace,
Born cosmonaut, tiny windhover
Of a spider, busy in its long trip,
On its gossamer trapeze
Spun out under the big top.

And, a giant at the performance,
I felt also the struggle, the near slip,
The scale, the insignificance,
What was given to things to sway
Through the world, the need to grip
Between the awful fall and the sky.

Fifth Rabbit

He rode in triumph on the carrier of our bike,
His ears giving the town the victory salute,
Death and dissection cheated at the eleventh hour;
His future—silly names, tickling, and food the like
No rabbit, even in nursery-land, had the right
To expect in the run of luck. The other four
Had now gone to the gas and the experiment,
Their futures cut and dried, needing no sentiment.

Yet he, his bacon saved, is hopping mad
That we should wire him in and make him fat;
And, no doubt, will soon try to burrow out
From salvation, and, alone, lose his head
To whatever preys on simple things
Which, being blest with scuts, cannot grow wings.

On Having a Poem Set for Examination

"Coleridge said: 'Poetry is the best words
In the best order.' Choosing one only
Of these poems, discuss this definition."

He was in the section 'On Beasts and Birds',
My rabbit—and what company to keep,
Rubbing rhyme-schemes with that tiger, those sheep!
Did any candidate pick the lonely,
Unpoetic pet, all scut and mere twitch,
No cause, like that snake, for much rhapsody?
No poem mine for the figures of speech,
The high style, to be learnt at home by heart
For testing the next day and for naming now;
No poesie mine for lovers to bow
Their itching heads to; no simplicity
Surprising among the fine excess;
No fine excess; no sublime quotation;
No flight to heaven with that albatross.

"State what you think the poem is about."

A rabbit. Only this and nothing more?
That raven is a symbol, and that lamb,
But what does this lowly one represent?
Do they not know who were scraping through
Examination memories for a few
Titbits in the big and silent room?
Did they not tell them who are taught to teach
The meaning familiar in ancient lore
Why a rabbit should at times consent
To take its place in heraldry and verse
With lions and with unicorns and such?

What is this life if full of cows
We have no time to watch a rabbit nibble
Fourteen flop-eared lines and hopping words—
Perhaps the best—defying famous birds
And beasts? Let him too have his finest hour!
I chose him. Let them about him scribble!
Besides, of all corpses in this fiction
Is not his most cut out for dissection?

Road Casualty

If it's squashed red, I swerve to the other side,
Minding my own business, passing the dead buck.
Someone will come and clean the guts from the road,
I assume, or the rain wash away the muck
That was once formed and shone with fur and, a wild
One, buffeted the land. A tidy end is bad
Enough, lying with paws crossed, its eyes cold
And still as marbles, run down and stiff as rock.
And so, since apparently it has to take
My way, where nothing grows for it, let it try
If it must be killed to do it without fuss,
Since, though I may wipe out a whole species, I,
Having this long journey to make through the dark,
Must not lose time, and swerving is dangerous.

Owl

Having heard it night after night for so long,
I decided to creep down the lane to the trees
And spy upon such screeching,
See at last this fierce disturber.
I matched myself against it,
My talents and its talons,
My stick and its beak,
My torch to light up its dark hide.
I moved towards a prey.

But it was not sharing any beam with me.
It cared too many hoots,
Denied itself a raid, went hungry to win.
And its patience lasted longer.
So, having only taken certain precautions,
And with no real heart in the game,
I went home with my guilt,
And waited to hear it again, no moper this one,
And was glad of the sound.

And I will not go a second time,
Not being wise enough to hunt with owls.

Cold Storage

Headless and hard as bricks, painted off-white,
Hanging like frozen clothes, the dead herd moves
Along the assembly-line to the street
Where, in the sawdust, butchers wait with knives.

Here is no slightest hint of buttercups
And daisies, bellowing and having calves,
And Lightfoot coming to the milking-shed.
Impossible also to think that shapes
Like these can grace the bodies of our loves
With softest skin and downy maidenhood.

Unlucky, then, for sacred three-in-one
We cannot correlate existences—
The rank-fat creature, the steak underdone
And oozing blood, and these clean carcasses.

Autumn: 1

Millions of crane-flies will spin autumn
To death in the clear time between the first mist
And the last, until, white-haired and blue-eyed,
The year lies mangered in innocence.
Mustard meadows will stretch across the hills,
Bubbling with leaves and worm-casts, the sky,
Dank with mortality, begin to smell
Of bonfires, and frost festoon the night.

How, then, shall the rigid soil comfort us
Who dream the future coming through the snow?
What, before it is too late, but carols
Can we sing to the flying ones and the wild
Weaving of the earth's shroud, as we walk
Long-legged over the yellow land?

Autumn: 2

That day everywhere was leaves,
The murky convention of autumn.
The fall moaned down the brown corridors,
And there was a lunatic look
In the eyes that passed me, mad boys,
Sad boys, come unwillingly
To a merely partial knowledge
Of what was wrong.

So I pushed through the procession
Towards winter, the lonely branches,
The frozen waiting.

And then, a star, one small boy smiled
Joy at me like a challenge,
And gospelled me a morning call.
He spoke, and his voice was a song,
And I took it up,
All the way to the upper room,
Early words, soaring to Spring
Beyond the feeble sun,
Poetry, all white, about nothing.

Grass

Older than monuments, poems will die
If no man comes across the levelled land
To dig the dead over and plant new songs
Among the eminent and mourning weeds.
But grass endures longer than bronze or words.
Dropped like mercy from bewildered wings
Beating back into the abandoned sky,
It explodes in huge silence underground.
And so it will happen, after the last
Bang, that in the radiating stillness
The wind will whistle grass to the ruins,
And fields creep like sunlight over the dust,
Until, green again and ripe for poetry,
The earth hops and singing men make hay.

Parrot Cry

As proud as Punch and Judy the parents left
Their idol with Nick, once their favourite pet
Until that boy had been born to usurp
The throne of the old swank who could shout
'Hell!' like the world's champion.

They would not be in church long, and Nick,
Having always been given the freedom of the room,
Would keep thieves out, for he proved
A demon with strangers, and, though seeming tame,
Would be a wild guard for their son.

So Nick was left to baby-sit for the first time,
And, being sportive, came and sat on baby, who laughed
To see such fun,
And grabbed and plucked a fine feather out;
And Nick, not to be beaten, stabbed his throat
And shouted 'Hell!'

    When they came back,
The parents found the young god spread
To his one wound, and, preening itself, the bird
Restored to its kingdom. By the door
The feather lay.

    Later, when
Nick was put to sleep by the vet, they shut him up
With the lost boy in a single tomb
That the two might rot together and share
The blame and the worship.

Inquest

He could not have been concentrating on his driving,
And the look of ecstasy on the girl's face
Hardly suggested that she herself had been behaving
As a lady should in public. Moreover,
The position from which the firemen and police
Extricated the pair was compromising,
To say the least, crushed in each other's arms,
Never before quite so close together—
Though how they managed it in so small
A car, especially behind the wheel,
Left the investigators guessing.

Yet, knowing all those daring young dreams
They had before mutilation, some of us
May not blame him if, for one long moment,
He took his eye off the future, the law
In both his hands, and looked his last on beauty.

Missing them now, all their brief fortune spent,
The road clean again, their heat gone to the fire,
How can we not be glad that they so blissfully
Were so unwise, laying down their lives
To be such friends? Needs must when the devil drives.

Pietà

(Garden of remembrance, early Spring, *in memoriam* a boy cremated)

Yet again, do what death may,
She stands like Mary at the sepulchre,
Bewildered lady, watching, wondering where
Her lord has gone. But no angels speak,
And no gardener comes.

Here she waits in her black hope
That he will appear, suddenly greeting,
The stone of sorrow rolled away,
All his lovely boyshape gathered back
From the flames and the sky.

And is there, then, a resurrection?
Who can there be for her to know and praise
After the burning and the scattering?
What can the wind through these trees blow
But dust into her eyes?

So we shall return in a year's time,
She to keep her rendezvous, and I
To keep her company and see
The garden rich with ash, and daffodils
Risen from the tomb.

Elegy

on a music-teacher whose home is to become a hostel for unmarried mothers

Long virgin years rehearsed her
For this silence;
All their lessons
Composed her to this ending.

So she lay in the songless room,
Folded and faded
Like her keyboard,
While men in black made notes.

Then, accompanied by flowers,
Pianissimo
The high solo
Bell played her in.

And now carpenters, with hammers
And radios
Loud in chorus,
Thump old scores into dust.

And here girls, out of harmony,
Their small crimes
In their arms,
Will come to practise lullabies.

Blackboard Jungle

nil nisi bonum

'Smith is dead, sir—killed yesterday after school. Did you know?'
My pupils jostled round me, all agog to tell me so.
Obviously they found this sudden end of one they knew, thrilling:
Life for a while was different in this killing.
How Smith died, what the car did to him and his bike,
Was the talk of the school that morning, the like
Of nothing on the telly or in sport;
Smith, for once and for all, had caught
The imaginations of his fellows, who never saw
Much to talk about in him before.
His form-mates wondered if he hadn't really come off best:
'Just like Smith to go and miss the Latin test.'

By dinner-time he was forgotten. Boys
At their allotted task with food no longer heard the voice
Of Smith crying from the wilderness of death.
They saved their breath
To cool their pudding.

            Three days later Smith was burnt.

I tell the tale, am not sure of the moral to be learnt:
Cruelty, thy name is childhood; ignorance is bliss—
Something of the sort perhaps.

               I add by way of postscript this:
(Overheard) 'I say, have you seen—you know where—the latest
    joke,
About how black Smith looked when he went up in smoke?'

Schoolmistress

Each day she takes the snotty bus to school,
Crammed with kids. Each evening she cleans
It out, sweeps up the aitches, mops the swill
Of syntax underneath the seats, then drains
The sums, washes away every mis-spelt word
From sticky windows, wipes the number-plate,
Reads the service-book, recites the highway-code,
Crosses herself, and drives into the night.

Asleep, she takes her chariot of fire,
Chauffeured by cherubs, escorted by stars.
Moons rise for her along The Milky Way;
The constellations curtsey; purity
Of sound from vast and silent skies she hears;
Gowned with goddesses, she rides the clear air.

R.I. Exam

The third-year boy, baffled by questions about God,
Held a tiny plastic skull for luck,
Starting young, hoping he was right;
Later, thinking what on earth to say,
He cuddled it. So they kept each other warm.

Once, in days further off from wishing,
It might have been St. Christopher whose back
Bore him to his master's good report,
Or a vernicle sewn upon his cap
To pardon all his errors with her charm.
But now it was his age's latest joke,
Sick as he was in his schoolroom flight
From knowledge. So he took possession
Of the favour to which he too must come;
And as I watched him struggling with the word,
And though I knew that time was on his side,
I saw the plaything blacken in his grip,
And death winking in his bright and early eye.

Henry Vaughan

We passed it, I like to think, at least three times
Before the lady told us that was the church;
And the sexton, tidying mortality,
Confirmed our quest—yes, sir, up there, at the back,
The only one with Latin on him—if
A soft Brecon laughter remembered right,
As though being so dead were here no great matter.

And we toured to the grave he had yearned for,
The useless servant, the greatest sinner;
Glory be to God and the Trinity
Of heads and snakes and the legend of the bread.

The sexton asked us the time as we came away,
Having, he still laughed, forgotten his watch,
As though that too did not matter any more
To him than the old hidden doctor
Who was also a poet, the little one
Strangled by coiling roots down to his bones,
Named in guide-books, ignored by the main road.

Shakespeare Among The Pigeons

Never was there a more nonchalant bard,
Leaning on a right elbow of fame,
Staring stonily at the stagey scene,
Careless of roar and useful to pigeons.
Who would have thought that man had so much verse
In so much foot-crossed languor, Osric-wise,
Holding his head so still when all around
Were turning theirs to the latest London?

But the place is good enough for an earl.
Let Leicester have his square to him preserved—
Mecca dancing, big screens and small buskers,
Taxis and tarts, and, in one corner smell,
The chestnuts they used to roast long ago.
Besides, is not the very atmosphere
That weathers him there rich with poetry,
All the men and women merely players
In his theatre? Is not his rival
No more than a name for a little space
Which by any other would look the same?

And so, with his tales and dreams behind him,
Winter and midsummer he leans on, waiting
In his artful fashion for such creatures
As the brave new world hath who come, eager
From the chartered sky, hot-foot for Stratford,
To tick him off their lists and consciences.

Nogoodboyo

He is no longer under the table or at the window, roaring a
    serenade,
Prone to lunge for a beer or a kiss on the balcony,
Metaphor-muzzy, simile-sick, attacked by alliteration.
His guitar is in the museum, the sounds he made
Are scattered influence over the future's poetry,
The strings are broken, the glasses smashed, the balcony in need
    of decoration.
Polly is back at the washing-up. Booze and beauty
Became again a very ordinary occupation.
Where did he go? You might ask the soil of Wales
For a secret or two. Better still, look into legend
And find him (who knows?) guzzling with goblins, the friend
Of every nymph, the Puck of the bunch, telling tales
About glare and gloom and glory, such as they were before he lay
Silent at last in the hospital that white November day.

Super-Tramp

He stumped the Georgian countryside to look
For sheep and cows to talk to and surprise
With all the wonders round about which they
Had never noticed even in the Spring;
Until, retired from jumping trains, he took
His meadow seat in green anthologies;
Respectable, he walked the pensioned way
To fame, where cuckoos, perched on rainbows, sang.

The rats missed his milk offering when he died,
The darkness came into its own again,
The fat, white monster fell into the sea;
And down in hell a lost soul, black with pride,
Its wooden leg unscrewed at last from pain,
Sat with contemptuous worms for company.

Cloud's Hill

(*T. E. Lawrence*)

Here he hung his banner on the outward wall,
Defying with a motto scratched in stone
The curse that, never more than one moment's
Throw away, patrolled these trees, would yell
His turn at last, and, with all its pistons
Firing across the flat, barren plain,
Bring death roaring up the lanes from Moreton.

Here he had come to dig himself out
Of the glory that swirled like a sandstorm
From the desert piled beyond this high hedge;
Here he built his rampart of books, wrote
Desperate despatches, lashed by rage,
Memorising ecstasy, the old shame
Pounding from records the key and the time.

Here, the nerve-centre of his secret war,
He kept his plan in bright working order,
Ready at a kick's notice for the road.
For soon, the demon at his back, he would hear
The trumpet sounded by the jolly lad,
Calling Boanerges, thunderous brother,
To take him on their last ride together.

At the Tomb of Oscar Wilde

I left behind the quick bread-and-wine streets,
And in the dead quarter, map-reading,
Reached, like any good English tourist, Oscar Wilde.

Egypt was still unmanned, then, though thrusting
Stiff among the alien tears; the faithful
And the outcast still scratched their homage
On the scandalous sculpture; and some young
Walker in the Magdalen shades had pencilled
'Oxford 1961'; a carnation
Lay on the ground nearby,
Button-holing the past.

And while, among the tombs, women pushed prams,
Lovers strolled with tomorrow on their lips,
And old men grew familiar with dust,
Beyond the trees the furnaces were hot,
And the chimney, flying its black pennant,
Declared its genius over Paris.

Protestant Cemetery

Tourists at the graves of Keats and Shelley

But what is it that makes them borrow time
From their catalogues of capitol and cross,
Bath and basilica, circus and bread,
To take these graves in their swift morning stride
Through the ruins and blessings of Rome?

Old quotations, is it, school memories,
Hauntings of mellow fruitfulness and clouds?
Or that, being mortal, they must warn the gods
Not to claim even this city for their own,
Since there's a richer dust concealed in this earth
Than settles on temples sacred and profane?

So the cemetery is ticked off, a debt to truth
And beauty paid. Guiltless, they take their seats
In gorgeous coaches, planning winter nights.

Advanced Level Poet

'Please go and put Lord Byron straight,'
I asked the boy sitting nearest the spot
Where the poet stood in his natty suit so nautical,
Leaning, as he never did alive, from the vertical:
You cannot, as he did, defy the deep blue sea and the devil
If you are not always strictly on the level,
And he had slipped, just a little, to the right.

Perhaps he had been pushed by someone who
Did not know how straightforward and true
He longed to be. Or perhaps the building moved,
Not realising how much he craved
The stillness it was never in him to attain.
So it was up to us to put him up again
Erect in his black frame, the line unbroken, as was his due.

He was, after all, one of the **A.L.** books.
With Juan the most owlish boys are gay as larks.
Let Chaucer have his swink to him reserved;
The problems of the *Hamlet* text unnerved
The most studious scholar; *A Shropshire Lad*
The whole group thought dangerous, mad and bad;
But Byron had distinction even in his looks.

Bunhill Fields

Pelted by pigeons, the end of his nose
Sliced off by a bomb straying from the war,
Boxed in by soaring glass and concrete,
John Bunyan lies, his mouldering stone
Not much to come for all this wintry way,
Such a literary progress, even
With Defoe and Blake thrown in the railings
For good measure. 'They're always taking
Pictures of him, sir, and everyone's a sinner.
Perhaps he remembered them in his will,
Left them something.' Then, greyness abounding,
He scuttled, guffawing, back to his hut
To keep warm, and I, not knowing why, returned
For a last look at the dirty figure,
One of the heirs, hounded by purity,
And left it to the curious glances,
Birds and whatever new wars might yet come,
And went into the big business world
Where John Wesley roared across City Road.

The Allegory of Love

When lovely women sit before the mirror
To change their hair and make other faces,
Eve's selves won by the watery image,
What chance have we of their devotion?

We lost our unity to them; they restore it
To their own keeping in daily ceremonial,
While we kneel in the dim lady chapel
And watch them celebrate their secrets.

Holy of holies, must we endure this?
Can we not claim back even what is ours?
See how we offer, hear how we sing,
We who are all their congregation.

Well, then, let them perform, entertain us
With their antic mysteries.
There is no service in an empty church,
No goddess where there is no praise.

One day, with their blessing, we shall go out,
Adam's selves into the wilderness,
Leave them here and find them there,
Not in hot windows or on cold walls

But in the moderate houses, row on row,
Where, after the feeding and the parables,
The washing of feet and the tempting,
We shall return with our vows to worship.

Antony and Cleopatra

They say she could drink him under the table
And leave him snoring in a pool of crumbs.
She beat him at billiards and had a bigger appetite,
And inspired better poetry.
It was, all things considered, an unequal match.
Rome understood it well, of course, and was angry.
A coloured queen was mightier than the sword,
Lust was stronger than the empire,
Love more lasting than the law;
The world was to be lost for plays.
It made nonsense of their skill with stones,
Their virtue, the mosaic truths.
So only one course was open: to strike while the passion was hot.
The boy Octavius girded up his cold loins
And struck the pair down,
And, avoiding any personal blame,
Returned to the hoarse, triumphant city.

Time and emperors passed.

Later, in a remote, occupied village
A farmer knocked up another stable,
And, looking south, their eyes on grandeur,
Restless hordes began to breed too fast.

Me and My True Love

So you take the high road, darling, and I the low,
Yours the nomad, mine the motor, way;
Yours too the sweet country lane, narrow,
With steep gradients, where you will meet stray
Customers, come almost to a complete stop
Behind holy herds, dread the mnemonic church,
Pass the time of day to strangers, need a map
And lose direction, panic and wind your watch.

I cannot halt on my road, emergencies
Excepted. All is plain speeding. The patrol car
Chaperons me; the breakdown gang, the police,
The ambulance wait for the inevitable hour.
Oh, I shall be there before you, darling, swift
As a shadow, my light winking to the left.

In the Post Office

Paying their weekly visit to the tomb, men
Play noughts and crosses with hope,
Fill the blank spaces of their lives
With vicious little circles,
Lay down their souls for dividends.
The supper of the last post
Is bitten from finger-ends,
The bitter beer drunk again,
Luck's chalice drained at one scoop,
Prayers offered for miracles.
Yet not a single Tom of them believes
He stands an unholy ghost
Of a treble chance. Sunday
Will not roll this stone away.

Market Day

I go gathering every Saturday
In the market-place, liking to listen
To the talkative, slapping salesmen,
See the lucky people, what is displayed
In the covetous garden, all lovely,
Mankind engaged in a roaring trade.

But I am looking for something else also,
Not to be found among the underwear,
The dead fish, the bare girls, the crocks,
The cut-price chocolates, the forgotten books.

Nor am I certain what it is, may
Not recognise it even there.
I just go, always go, must go,
Every Saturday, the unreal day between
The pay-packet and the essential work,
Between the dying and the disappearance.
On the off-chance I steal back
Like Adam to the gates with rusty hands.

Out-Patient

Leaving the clinic, not caring to be in,
I went, wading, to the impatient
River, which wasted no time, chucked dead wood,
And let birds show what they were made of,
Stern stuff against the tide.

We were in boatless winter, and the hospital
Offered no solution; it was the river gave
Pledges to whatever fought its surface.

So I preferred its suddenness
To white coats and the patching of my pain.
I was in a February mood,
Wanting the water smells, not the scent
Of wards, wanting to be out. My racing tail
Was up, and I dabbled towards the ocean.

All Those Things

Far removed from there, beside the seaside
Or near the still unvisited temple,
Doing nothing or travelling the road
That winds up above the snow to simple
Brush-strokes or notes or words which hint at truth;
Idle with nature or contemplating
The mystery of her miles, all this growth
Of strange, new creatures for ever greeting
Me as though surprised to see me again—
When I am not there, I think of those things
Which, never alive, live only as mine,
Bits of me left behind waiting like songs
To be sung in praise of my good return,
My portable property that is me at home,
Switched off, shut up, at rest, making no sound.
And I am impatient, here above ground,
To go back, let the air in, flesh their bones
And listen to their old and seemly tunes.

As Instructed

I chose my own from the offerings,
As instructed.
There were all the kinds to wonder with,
Shades of meaning, degrees of hope,
But I knew the one.

Then I breathed into it my songs,
As instructed.
And I thought it comely,
And I gave it a name,
First in the world.

That was long ago. I turned elsewhere,
As instructed.
Out of sight and mind, it sank,
Abandoned with old fancies,
Keeping darkness.

Until, one day, searching,
As instructed,
I found it in the dust of that time,
Not soft as in the beginning,
Stiff as crosses.

I listened for any whispering,
As instructed,
But heard nothing. So I threw it
In the fire, and watched my childood
Flare for ever.

Night

Lying here behind the years, I watch
The gathering of the rare possessors,
Each in its magical and timid place;
They swell in the darkness, prepare themselves
To go with me, shadows, in procession
Through cloisters to the passionate cells.

And there, meeting the dead, we mock
This room and the coming back of light.
Our black business must be done again
Inside the broken walls, about the slabs.
We float in ages of gloom
Towards some stupendous dread. Until,
And always elsewhere, big bells,
High in the night's sinister cathedral,
Toll for another day's forgetting.

Chiaroscuro

Here are the very temples of delight,
Mammon's basilicas, brash and bright,
Where pin-up frescoes celebrate The Fall,
Saint Priapus triumphant on each wall.
Here hidden choirs, with hot antiphony,
Beat and twang the unholy litany
In cheeky chancels indirectly lit.
Here the black-as-midnight ladies sit.

Once in Padua, a tourist day,
I stood in the coloured dimness, alone
With silent pilgrims come to touch the cold
Sarcophagus and see the teeth, the bone,
The tongue still uncorrupted in the gold
Reliquary. And there little friars pray.

Strip Club

Sweetly disordered, the dresses drop
Like waterfalls down each creviced back
To shimmer, pools of silk, on the bawdy floor:
Then, with cheeky, Charleston flick,
High heels heave them to the laundry
In the wings, and the girls gleam, pinned up
For the business, advertising underwear
And long legs. So, modelling, slowly
They unwind their pink selves to the travellers
Who, land-locked with the same wives in every
Port, watch jewelled hands crawl like crabs across
Breasts, and fingers, small truncated men,
Scuttle up thighs, those dark peninsulas,
To unhitch and unroll the nylon skin,
At last untie the tantalising knot.

The naked Eves stand, still and spotlit,
Observing decorum with a cute wink,
Briefly clapped and vanishing in the moist
Blackness of the room; and the old Adams,
Who have paid so lavishly to see
What oft they've seen but ne'er so well undressed,
Wake up from their evening-out dreams
And take their solitary way to the bar
To swap and drown their weakness in strong drink.

Apron Stage

And 'tis said they made themselves aprons,
And lo, there was the first dust
To be swept under the carpet, the first
Morning ashes to be cleaned, sons
To beget in the first shame,
The scene to be set for the first crime.

So Adam took her to a bed of flowers,
Took her in the flowers, and Eve knew
Him not, the unfamiliar man who
Ravished her now. Terrible years
Of mothering stretched ahead,
And in her horror she was proud.

Nor did Adam know himself. What
Was this new and huge desire?
They did not tell him, the higher
Ones who flew down, garbed in white,
To comfort and warn him, that this
Was the primal wickedness.

Helpless, like the strange seasons, he went
To her again. And, in her fullness, Eve,
The time come, gave birth beside her grave.
And it came to pass that death, obedient,
Parted them, knowing the way, having found
A trail of slime along the modest ground.

Uncle

My sainted uncle left us only the glum face
In the cupboard, and his young sins,
For souvenirs. He had gone from bad
To worse, and was good for nothing;
And he had sailed away over the sea
With only persecution for a friend,
To make his fortune or be broken,
His feet in chains or golden sandals.

Long silence suggested chains, until
Letters began to come, one or two a year,
Progress reports. He was growing rich,
Thought we might like to know about it,
Hoped we were well, and sent his love.

But suddenly he stopped writing. We assumed
He was dead, and locked the cupboard door.

Then, out of the blue he flew in,
A roaring stranger, wearing golden sandals,
Gigantically haloed, good for anything.
And, after the wining and the dining,
He confessed he was a prodigal, had returned
To expiate those sins and tear
That glum face from our history.
He was glad we were well, and loved us all.

And now, mere tenants in our own house,
We remember an invasion, no visit:
We became an occupied territory.

Black-eyed Teenager

As we passed each other in the bad street
He stared at me with his one open eye
Like a challenge, demanding satisfaction.
I thought of gangs and brawls and cruel slogans,
Offensive weapons, disturbing the peace;
But then wondered: perhaps his great ideals
Had brought him such a badge of courage,
Such a stigma, defending to the death his own.
Young man, I said, you are once more the prototype.
Gone are the halfway boys, the middlemen,
Returned are the black and white, the all or nothing,
The for or the against. You are angel or devil,
And your swollen, proud slit of blindness
Means only one of two things, both terrible:
Either your jacket hides your fledgling wings,
Or your shoes hide your cloven hooves.
Where, then, is the itching, where the pain?
Between your shoulder-blades or in your feet?

Triumvirate

Once, almighty Caesar wore a careless gown,
And slapped his sandals on a dolphined floor,
Clicked his fingers, banged his palms, and conjured men,
Servants of the god, out of nowhere.
He committed glory, personified sin,
And did it all with a natural flair;
He took himself to be a lord of life,
Never doubted he was a beast with a brain,
Sentenced towns to death, had womanhood for wife;
And when he died the streets were packed with grief.

Later, the proud duke, robed in merchandise,
Used beauty to prove that he was right,
And, doubting himself, patronised the wise,
Consecrating his power to delight,
Concealing his faithlessness in galleries,
Walling up his guilt in palaces of art.
He lived an absolutely splendid lie
Told by everyone about him; no price
For golden domes and duchesses was too high;
And when he died all gasped at such a passing by.

Now, the big boss, anonymously dressed,
Cups a microphone between his veneered hands
And dictates from a concrete throne the latest
Monologue. He is millions of minds,
The private man with the public voice raised
To a grey, air-conditioned eminence.
He presides over filing cabinets;
Glory and power are his means to ends
He measures out, like love, in programmed notes;
And when he dies commuters raise their hats.

Time

Well, Ralph, you can, I suppose, hope to halt
A caravan just for one day. Perhaps
A gipsy can be tempted by poetic gifts,
Not least sweet girls to festoon him with may.
And there are sterner ways to slow him down:
Police traps, ramps, squatters in the road,
Tranquillisers for him and his jennet.
Or you might steal his whip or put a bomb
Underneath his black and polished wheels.

Oh, I do not blame you, Ralph, for wishing.
Do not I too share the white symptoms?
Are not the feasts and saints hounding me
Always with newer years and offerings?

But, Ralph, I ask you, man to ghost,
What hope, what wishing, or what poetry—
Souls burning out across a cold sky—
Can halt a warrior in his winged chariot?

Poetry

It is the roaring drives us out again
Through the formal avenues to the wilderness
Of no trails, the long growths,
Shedding our load, keeping only
The best order possible
Until we reach
A clearing.
And

Then
All we
Can do is
Retreat from the gap
Between where no words are
And their final arrangement, and make
Our way back past the beautiful temptations
To the starting point, and the silence calling.

Biographical Notes

Julian Ennis was born in 1915, and went to The King's School, Chester. From 1934 to 1937 he was at Merton College, Oxford, where he read English, with Edmund Blunden and John Bryson as his tutors. Then he spent a year at the Oxford Department of Education, and became a teacher. Long afterwards, in 1972, he retired early from the post of Head of the English Department in a boys' grammar school; and in 1976 he moved to Sidmouth in East Devon.

He has edited school textbooks, notably anthologies of verse; he made the Panther paperback selection of the poems of Thomas Hood (1970); he has contributed critical and research articles to several periodicals; and he has had a selection of his own poems, *Cold Storage*, published, also in 1970, by Pergamon Press. Some of these poems are republished in this book, but usually in revised versions. Some, too, have been recorded by The British Council, and by ARGO for the series, *The Poet Speaks*.